I'M ONLY HERE FOR THIRTY DAYS

TONYA WILSON

Copyright © 2021. Tonya Wilson

All rights reserved. Printed in the U.S.A.

No part of this publication may be reproduced or transmitted in any form or by any means, electronic or mechanical, including photocopy, recording or any information storage and retrieval system now known or to be invented, without permission in writing from the publisher, except by a reviewer who wishes to quote brief passages in connection with a review written for inclusion in a magazine, newspaper or broadcast.

DEDICATION

To my children Khaliq and Jalil Abdul-Latif and the many role models, I had over the years that made me who I am today. I love you all and will forever remain in deep gratitude for the life I have been provided.

Table of Contents

LETTER FROM THE AUTHOR..6

CHAPTER ONE 9

CHAPTER TWO 16

CHAPTER THREE 21

CHAPTER FOUR 26

CHAPTER FIVE..30

CHAPTER SIX 35

CHAPTER SEVEN 38

CHAPTER EIGHT 45

CHAPTER NINE 49

CHAPTER TEN 54

CHAPTER ELEVEN 59

CHAPTER TWELVE 63

CHAPTER THIRTEEN 68

CHAPTER FOURTEEN 76

CHAPTER FIFTEEN 80

CHAPTER SIXTEEN 85

CHAPTER SEVENTEEN 92

CHAPTER EIGHTEEN	97
CHAPTER NINETEEN	104
CHAPTER TWENTY	109
CHAPTER TWENTY-ONE	112
CHAPTER TWENTY-TWO	115
CHAPTER TWENTY-THREE	119
CHAPTER TWENTY-FOUR	124
CHAPTER TWENTY-FIVE	129
ABOUT THE AUTHOR	134

LETTER FROM THE AUTHOR

The purpose of this book is to reach all youth with diverse backgrounds, giving alternative ways to cope with the challenges of life. This book will not only inspire you to keep pushing through but will also provide direction on how to go about getting what you need to succeed.

Working on this book has been a long journey. As you can see, I'm Only here for 30 Days is the edited Edition of "A Way Out" published in 2013. This is how long the journey has been. In 2013, when I first published my story, I knew it was important, but I didn't understand the real importance until after I hit submit and the book was published.

A Way Out was written and produced as a diary but was not effective in the way that it needed to be. So, believe me, when I say all things get better with time, they do. Now, fast-forwarding 2021, we have I'm Only Here for 30 Days. Nevertheless, it took time and patience to get to the result. It took strength to even gather my thoughts to write. There were times when I cried, laughed, and even became overwhelmed, but I needed to do this. I felt an overwhelming desire to help, inspire, and motivate others like myself from similar backgrounds.

Growing up in foster care was not easy to endure. I remember when I arrived at my first group home; I was given a diary to record my thoughts. Once I mastered how to use it, I started writing everything down. I wrote everything from my thoughts to how my day went. Then as

I entered my adult life, I realized that I couldn't stop, because life was still happening. Writing is soothing to me; it teaches me a lot about myself because I can't help but read what I write which offers me another perspective every time.

Imagine an over 25-year-old married woman with children proudly toting around several notebooks and diaries. I think my husband at the time thought I was crazy when he saw PLEASE DO NOT READ along with other threats in bold letters plastered all over the front of them. No, I'm sure it's my insecurity.

Carrying those totes around every time we had to move got me thinking. Then, I realized I had been carrying my childhood story around in a tote for years. I had been toting it physically, mentally, and emotionally. It was simply too much. So not only did I decide to write this book to begin to heal myself and to share my story with the world; most importantly this book is meant to be used to offer a distinct perspective on the foster care system, at-risk youth, homelessness, parenting and life itself.

At-risk youth need to have real people with diverse backgrounds demonstrate for them what it is to lead a positive life. Progressing in the foster care system was a challenging task for me as an adolescent. Learning ways to take a step back and look at me first, then take small steps to change my flaws was the hardest. Childhood trauma breeds infections, it's up to you to provide the coping antibiotic. If you don't heal now and move on, you will carry this baggage over into your adult life, it's best to work through the challenges as they come. No more holding everything inside, other people need to know that they are not alone and that there is always another way.

I had the opportunity to experience both sides of being in foster care and then as an adult working in the field of Social Work. It has given me insight and perspective on both ends.

Finally, use your life experiences as the blueprint for your success. If you've had any challenging experiences in your life, then you already know right from wrong. You know the difference between what a good feeling is vs a bad feeling. Just because you feel your parents or other adults failed you does not give you the right or excuse to make poor choices and decisions. Be who you are meant to be and not who you have been accustomed to. Use your common sense and stop and think of the consequences of your actions first.

I'M ONLY HERE FOR THIRTY DAYS

Chapter 1

At the age of seven years old my siblings and I lived with Grandma Kalette in the city of St. Louis, Missouri. Grandma Kalette's house was huge it was a two-story brick home down in the city on N. Market St. Grandma Kalette turned her dining room into a bedroom for us and she converted her living room space into a bedroom for herself.

The un-kept house was overflowing with family; three aunts, four cousins, and a friend of the family, and her daughter was living in the basement. Most nights my mother was out. On those nights, mother would always come in with a raging temper and a particular passion for the discipline. Due to severe drug abuse and torment from her past, my mother was unstable. When my mother would be out late, Grandma Kalette took care of us. Unfortunately, I was a frequent bedwetter, to say the least.

One night while I was sleeping, I had another accident. As I laid there, I became cold in my yellow nightgown, it was soaked from head to toe. Feeling ashamed about my inability to control my bladder, I looked to my grandmother for help with my puppy dog eyes. I got up and tipped toed across the floor to Grandma Kalette's room. I was shivering with no socks on my feet. I could tell my grandmother was upset with me by the frown on her face as I entered her room. However, knowing my mother's tyrannical temper she tried to get me clean before my mother came home.
She said, "Ga-al you wet yourself again, yo momma gone tare yo tail up if she sees you, come on and get out of those pissy clothes." As she unzipped the back of my gown it was too late. I could hear the heavy squeak of the front

door opening. My heart started to pound; I could hear the pounding of my heart.

My mother was already coming through the front door and right into my grandma's room. Her furious big brown eyes looked at me, and then glanced at my grandmother as she slowly realized that I had pissed on myself again. I mean, I didn't even get to sneak any water that night and I still pissed. My grandma looked down at the floor shaking her head. I looked up and glared at my mom from the side, all I could see was her standing in the doorway swaying with her hands pressed to her medium-built hips. I turned to grandma to help me; all I could see was her tilted head of grey hair looking down at the floor as she sat on the edge of her bed. The tears started to roll down my face, I was soaked in urine and about to receive another traumatic whooping.

She said, "yeah, you finna get yo ass whooped."

Mother didn't have a belt this time. Instead, she scoured the house for something to beat me with. My heart pounded feverishly; fear took over my small body. I jumped up and down with my single ponytail swinging back and forth, shouting repeatedly "No please don't whoop me, I won't do it again I promise." The only thing that was on my mind was, run or stay? I kept telling myself, yes you can do it, you can take it, don't run. I stayed. She found a suitable cord, then grabbed me by one arm and started whipping me as she hollered her usual unintelligible threats that I never seemed to remember the next day. The beating continued until she became tired.

Thank God it's over, I thought to myself. Mother sat down and took a breather, then told me to take my clothes off. I paused my crying and assumed that the painful lashing to my damped brown skin was over and that it was time for me to change my clothes. As I stripped down to my underwear, mother became even more upset as she saw the damage done to my grandmother's couch. Enraged, she searched for another tool to beat me with. Scared and extremely frightened, I took off running up the stairs. My cousins hid me under their full-sized bed in their bedroom. Her booming footsteps could be heard coming up the stairs, as she looked for me.

"I'm going to beat the hell out of you," she yelled.

Her footsteps got closer to my cousins' room and she walked in. The room was silent.

"Where she at?"

My cousins were busy preparing for school, and I didn't hear them tell her where I was. However, when I looked up, she was glaring down at me.

"Get yo ass from under there now, you little B****!"

As her words pierced my heart, I kept trying to figure a way out. I refused to come from under the bed. She raced to the other side of the bed, and I slid away across the cold hardwood floors. Every time Mother moved to one side of the bed; I would desperately move to the other. She couldn't get to me, but the feeling was short-lived. She moved the bed and flipped the mattress. I could see my cousins' standing around in fear as she demanded them to hold the mattress and box spring up. Then, she grabbed the jar from the dresser and threw it at me.

"No!" I screamed repeatedly, as I tried to cover my head as the jar hit the floor and shattered into tiny pieces, slicing into my skin.

Terrified and shaking, I didn't move. At this point, I thought I wouldn't survive. I was petrified.

Mother yanked me by my single ponytail, pulled me from under the bed while dragging me over the glass pieces on the floor and down the stairs. There, I was beaten with an extension cord, as she scowled and said she was going to kill me for running.

"This is too much," my grandmother repeated to my mother as she started to clean my cuts. I was in so much pain that I could not stop shaking or crying. Wistful tears trekked down my cheek, too afraid to even look at my mother as she walked out the door. Sadly, I grew angrier with myself. No matter how hard I tried I still wet the bed. I ended up missing a few weeks of school until my wounds healed.

Chapter 2

Early one morning, my sister and I were getting ready for school, we both were fatigued. Mother had been awake all night. She and Carl laid on the bed together watching television and drinking, laughing loud enough that the whole house could hear. Our beds were right on the side of mother's bed so we could hear them all night as they continued this drunken obnoxious behavior. Danny and I couldn't sleep. Our lack of sleep caused us to move like sloths. Of course, this angered mother. Startling us out of bed, mother hurried us with her gut-wrenching threats.

"Get up and put your uniforms on," she barked. "I told ya'll to get dressed. If you are not dressed in the next few minutes, I'm going to whup both of you!"

Danny and I were so nervous. We scrambled to find our uniforms in a panicky fear, Danny unknowingly put on my uniform, and I slipped into hers. Mother grabbed the extension cord and swatted Danny with her merciful less tool first. Frightened, I tried to put my clothes on. I nervously waited for my turn. My baby sister Latrice began crying as she watched from the tub, resulting in mother swatting her a few times with the cord as well. She was on a rampage. Unable to control the urge, I ran to get as far away from her as possible. I could feel that she wasn't finished with Danny and me. I ran through the house and as I made Aunts Sinn's bedroom. She yelled.

"Don't come in here!" As she stormed into her room and shut the door, but I couldn't resist. There was nowhere else to run and hide. I panicked and ran inside and closed the door. My Aunt shook her head and continued to watch television. I ran and hid behind her dresser under all the dirty clothes that were behind there.

I heard her coming towards my Aunt's bedroom. I immersed myself a little deeper under the piles in fear that she would find me at any moment. She opened the door and closed it. Moments passed, I said to myself "Thank God she didn't check." My mother continued to yell for me repeatedly.

I wondered what I was going to do if she came back? I knew I couldn't take the beating she was about to give me, I wouldn't. In a split-second decision, I opened the second-floor window, just as I started to climb out, I heard mother reentering my Aunt's door. I saw my mother's face and I looked down at the distance of the concrete.

"Tonya, NO!" Aunt Sinn yelled.

Mother grabbed the back of my shirt and pulled me back into the room. She beat me till the blood leaked out of my welts. I broke away again, this time I ran down the steps, then into the basement. I hid behind the washing machine, the chilling scream of my name rang through the house. I felt horrified and afraid for my life. The cobwebs and cold concrete made me shiver. She enlisted Danny to help find me then ransacked the basement, turning on every washing machine. Finally, she found the one I was hiding behind and powered it on. I flinched, and she heard me.

There was no getting away. As many times before, Mother pulled me by my hair, dragged me up the stairs, and beat me until she was tired again. The painful lashes to my skin, legs, and back felt like pins and needles being pierced into my skin repeatedly. After it was over, I'd obtained even more welts all over my legs. The painful sores on my legs bled unyieldingly. I was forced to stay in my bedroom within the house for days and was not allowed to attend school. My childhood was filled with an array of cruel punishments for fickle matters such as those.

Severe beatings such as the time when I took a pack of

Kool-Aid from my Aunty Sinn, that ensued welts and bruises from the use of a rubber shower rope and being confined to my grandmother's home for weeks until my wounds healed.

TONYA WILSON

Chapter 3

It was a warm day outside, I had awakened from a nap in my mom's queen-size bed, in the back bedroom on the second floor of my grandma's house. I was still dressed from that morning in my blue jean shorts and a short sleeve pink tee shirt. I had my worn dingy white girl sneakers on. I could hear the news on my Aunt Annie's television in the next room, so I knew that her door was open. I got out of bed and headed into the bathroom to cross over into her room, as I got to the hallway by the stair's I noticed my Aunt Sinn's boyfriend Terence creeping up the stairs. Terence was an older guy in his late 50's with a head full of white-greyish hair. He always wore a cap. I was confused when I saw him, I couldn't figure out why he would be carrying a gun. I had never seen one up close before.

I proceeded into my Aunt Annie's room to see what she was doing. She was laying on the bed watching TV. Terence went down the hall into my Aunt Sinn's room, before I could sit on the bed all I could hear was my Aunt Sinn asking Terence what he was doing in a relaxed but terrified tone. My Aunt Annie turned the TV down then I could hear my Aunt Sinn telling him to put the gun down. I stepped back into the hallway and my Aunt Annie continued to sit on the bed, I guess she figured it was just another argument. I saw my Aunt Sinn leap and grab the gun and try to take it away from him, the lights were off, and the only light was the sun beaming in from the outside. My Aunt's bed was close to the door and I could see the hall by the stairs.

My aunt Sinn and Terence tussled back and forth slamming each other into the walls and the balcony. I was terrified as I stood there helpless, and screaming to my Aunt Annie to help. My Aunt Annie rolled over and started to slip into her slippers as the tussling and togging entered her room.

She yelled, "Tonya go to your room" y'all got to get out of my room." She was stunned as she saw the gun that they were pulling back and forth in her room, she screamed, "No don't kill my sister! Not in front of the kids, Terence," she repeated.

My hands were shaking and sweaty as my heart pounded heavily. I didn't know what to do. I headed back into my room, I tried to figure out what to do. I can't let him hurt my Aunt. I could hear him slamming my Aunt Sinn up against the wall in my Aunt Annie's room. I remember that my mother always kept a bat in our room, but I wasn't sure exactly where it was, so started to search for it. As I searched, I heard my Aunt Annie tell Terence that she was getting ready to call the police if he didn't leave. I stopped looking for the bat and peeked from the bathroom. He wasn't saying anything he just had a spaced-out look on his face the entire time they tussled back and forth. After he heard my Aunt say she was calling the police, he let her go, and tucked his gun into his pants, and headed back down the stairs. My Aunt Sinn stood there in my Aunt's room in her torn black tee-shirt, her blue jeans were halfway down, and she was barefoot. She didn't seem to be bothered by what just happened, she apologized to my Aunt Annie for the hole in her wall. My Aunt Annie was so upset with her ignoring what she had to say, she immediately got on the phone and called my Aunt Nita to tell her about what happened. My Aunt Sinn went into her room and closed the door. I saw my sister Danny coming up the stairs, she could tell by the horrifying look on my face that something bad happened. She said, "What's wrong with you, what happened?" I told her that Terence came into the house with a gun and jumped on Aunt Sinn, she immediately called my dad Lonnie, who at the time was living around the corner. He wasn't home but my oldest brother Lil Lonnie's girlfriend Nikki was the only one at home. Danny explained to her what happened, and she told us, to sit tight and she would walk around to our house to get us. Meanwhile, the house next door was being kicked in by the police. The neighbors from down the street were all standing around watching what was going on, Danny and I packed a small bag and waited for Nikki's arrival.

Use everything that you have witnessed as a key to success instead of a hindrance. Don't internalize the negative because somewhere in the negative there is a positive.

TONYA WILSON

Chapter 4

After Terrence tried to kill my aunt, I was relieved that my sister Danny showed up. It took a while for Nikki to arrive because she had to walk to get us and she had her baby with her. The police were still next door searching and bringing things out of the house. I couldn't figure out what the big deal was because my aunts were always over there and there were always random people running in and out. The neighbor's house was known as the "crack house" on the block, the house appeared to be vacant but a lot of people were always there. When Nikki arrived she didn't come inside the house, she waited for us to get our things. I kissed my Aunt Annie and told her that we were heading over to our dads. Aunt Annie sat on the side of the bed, she told us to be careful and that she would see us later. The block was crowded, and everyone was out on their porches.

It was hot outside. We saw our cousins on our way out. They were running to see what happened. My cousin Tasha was more worried about when we were coming back until I told her about what Terence did. She ran into the house looking for her mom, Danny and I went up the street. On the way to my dad's house, I talked about what took place in detail to Nikki. She could not believe what happened, she kept saying "it's okay Tonya, I am so sorry you had to see that." I couldn't get the images out of my head I was still shaking and I would get even madder every time I had to tell the story.

We made it to the house. My stepmom Caroline was home and my step-sister Connie. After getting settled, Nikki went ahead and told the story, so I wouldn't have to again. I went and laid down on the couch. I could hear Caroline yelling "Oh my goodness. This is enough! These kids shouldn't be going through this." Caroline was loving and passionate. Although she and my father hadn't been together for a long time, she still loved us as her own. Her reaction was normal. I continued to watch cartoons on the TV in the living room. When my dad called Caroline she told him what happened. He asked to speak to me, I picked up the phone that was hanging next to the refrigerator. He asked me if I was okay. I told him that I was fine, he told me about a new video game that he bought and asked me if I wanted to play the game. I loved playing video games and being at Caroline's house.

Caroline's house was beautiful. It was a very spacious four-bedroom home with three levels. It was the biggest house I had ever seen. It was made of orange bricks and had a white fence around it. It sat on the corner. It was extremely comfortable and peaceful. I went to Caroline's room after I talked to my dad. She was laying across the bed in her bright-colored flower sundress. I had just enough room as always to ball up underneath her, I liked to be closed to her, she always smelled like lavender and had a natural scent. I balled up and watched TV with her, she rubbed my ponytail and decided what hairstyle she was going to style my hair. I remembered the game that my father mentioned and I headed downstairs to play the game until my dad returned from work.

Don't let someone else's mistakes cause you not to recognize the mistake and motivate your growth.

I'M ONLY HERE FOR THIRTY DAYS

Chapter 5

After we moved out of my grandmother's house, we moved into a property that my Aunt Naple owned. It was a small house. It had a one-bedroom and was it was extremely hot and sticky inside.

We lived there during the week and on the weekends, we stayed with my dad. We later moved into a new house with my mother and we didn't have anyone to talk to there. The electricity wasn't on and at night I would get anxious because I was afraid of the dark. My sisters Latrice and Danny were also afraid of the dark. During the day, my mother would sleep and be out all night. There were times that we didn't eat, the only available thing to eat was peanut butter. I remember my siblings and I would dig out big spoons of peanut butter for breakfast and sometimes dinner. My mother cooked delicious meals, although dinner was slim to none. I remember feeling comfortable when she would be in the kitchen cooking. During the day we would entertain ourselves by playing games or sleeping. I especially enjoyed hiding for hours until I went to sleep.

During the summer it was too hot for us to do anything outside. When I got bored I would rock in my mom's recliner and sing, "I want my mommy, I want my daddy, I want my sisters." This was very soothing to me. Danny took on the responsibility of looking after us and she would get in trouble if something happened.

One night during the summer when mother was out, we lit a candle to see out of the security bars on the locked door. We weren't allowed outside when she wasn't home, and the only action we'd partake in was looking outside and watching the other kids across the street play.

One night, my sisters and I were looking out of the bars; mother told us she would be back soon. Danny and I could see her walking up and down the street. She was pacing as if she was waiting on someone. There were bushes and trees planted in the front yard where the gate was and the house sat on a hill.

Danny and I sat on our knees as we looked down our block at the activities taking place. People would be out throughout the night, walking up and down the street. My mother was friendly with the neighbors and she would be yelling up and down our block as she paced. Suddenly, two guys pulled up, stepped out of a black car, and walked up to Sheryl. They appeared to be arguing, I could see my mom putting her hands up and trying to walk away then I heard, "Where is my money, B****?"

Then one of the guys got behind mother and grabbed her hair and told her that she wasn't going anywhere. She kept saying, "okay man, damn okay," while the other man pulled out his gun. He said, "now, I am going to ask you again." He shouted, "where is my money, B****? I told you to have my money."

All I could do was yell, "please don't hurt my mommy!" through the bars but they couldn't see nor hear us. Danny made my baby sister and I lay down on the floor and close our eyes. She put her hands over my mouth when I screamed.

The men took Mother down the street out of our sight. Danny said, "she couldn't see them anymore." We didn't know what happened to her, we were worried, and anticipating for her to walk in the door. It was too hot I couldn't sleep that night, Danny made us get into bed, we had all seen enough for the night.

No matter what the hardship is, do the best that you can do, be the best person you can be. Your future is what you make it no matter what you have experienced or where you have been.

Chapter 6

My mother came into the house after we had fallen asleep, early the next morning. She looked disoriented, her head was slightly bleeding, and she acted as if nothing happened. We all sat up and gave her hugs. I felt a feeling of relief. I had woken up in the middle of the night, peeked out the window, and prayed that mother would return soon, we were glad that she had. At that moment, we heard pounding on the door and men yelling to my mother to let them in, before they break the door down. My mother was in a daze. She had a blank stare on her face, her hair wasn't combed, which was very unusual.

She went to the door and opened the door for them. They came in and noticed my sisters and me sitting up on the bed. They took a glance at each other and continued to threaten Mother. The three of us slowly huddled up to one side of the bed and then gradually moved into the corner between the wall and the bed. I was afraid that they would hurt us too, they continued to shout horrible words at mother.

They ram-shacked the apartment, throwing clothes and knocking over the only table lamp we had; they threw the end table up against the wall across from the bed and they searched the nightstand drawers. Mother stood there helplessly in silence and seemingly afraid of the unknown, by the terrified look on her face.

She kept saying repeatedly, "a'ight man!"

The big heavy-set guy shouted repeatedly, "B**** where is my money!", as the other guy hemmed her up against the wall.

They had gold teeth and wore black leather hats. The men were both dark-skinned, tall, and heavy build with buck teeth. My sisters put our heads down in the corner, she peeked out and tears rolled down our faces. The brutal men held mother at gunpoint, yelling, and screaming out harsh words until they exited the house. The house was torn up, it looked like we had been robbed, even though they didn't take anything. After the incident, my mother held us until we all fell asleep. But when we woke up, she was gone.

The more you speak the easier the healing can take place.

Chapter 7

Awaken by hot and sticky sheets being gently tugged by Latrice, as all three of us laid in mother's bed. Mother had been gone most of that day and we were hungry.

Danny and I found a jar of peanut butter for us to eat in the cabinet, mother would always get it from the local food pantry when food was low. We would sit on the floor in the kitchen with three spoons and eat until we got full. It kelp us from being hungry for an hour or two throughout the day.

Danny managed to get in contact with my dad. He came over before he went to work. We watched him as he got out of his van. He walked up the stairs in his black casual shoes and he wore a short-set, a hat with a feather in it, and he had a box of chicken in his hand. He talked to us and fed us fried chicken through the bars on the door. I could tell that he was furious by his bloodshot eyes and the sweat dripping down his dark-complexion face but, I couldn't help but wonder why he couldn't get us out. He couldn't believe that we were locked in the house behind bars with no way to get out. He said, "he had to go to work and that he would see us later, and have a talk with our mom." We knew we would get to see him the weekend.

Most of the day was filled with playing games and running through the house. That evening, I rocked back and forth in my sky-blue rocking chair repeatedly singing "I want my momma, I want my daddy, I want my sisters" over and over again, as the sun went down, I fell asleep. It was an everyday routine; it was soothing to me. However, it annoyed Danny but I had no care in the world.

Latrice was up still roaming around when I awakened from my nap. She was only three years old at the time. My sister Danny lit a candle and sat it next to the bed before she went to sleep. I was sitting in the rocking chair when I heard Latrice screaming. I could smell something burning. I jumped up and ran into the room where Danny was and she jumped up. Latrice was rolling on the bed holding her head. Danny realized that she had left the candle too close to the bed and start panicking.

"We are in trouble, we are in trouble," Danny repeated.

She jumped out of bed and ran to the kitchen, while I tried to look at Latrice's hair. I saw a patch of hair burned out and a piece of the candle's wax melted into her hair. It appeared that the candle had only irritated her scalp just a little.

Danny came back with a cold towel to apply to Latrice's scalp. Latrice would not allow her to do so. She started screaming and kicking. We decided to let her calm down and then try again. Danny picked her up and rocked her until she drifted off to sleep. After Latrice was asleep, Danny washed her hair with the towel and then combed the candle wax out of her hair. I was so nervous, I thought that our apartment was going to be buried that night. Danny yelled at me for falling asleep and not playing with her. I told her that we should have been watching her and this wouldn't have happened. We both knew that we were going to get a beating when mother came back home.

We sat at the front door behind the bars, watching the streets, awaiting our mother's arrival. Later that night Latrice woke up and she was back to normal. She was laughing and wanting to play. Mother walked up the stairs and she saw us in the doorway, she yelled, "get out the damn door." We backed up like the three stooges and waited for her reaction at the sight of Latrice's bald spot. She lit more candles to brighten the room. She said, "What the hell happened?" Danny and I started talking at the same time, we were nervous as we explained what happened.

Mother said, "Shut up!" "Tonya tell me what happened." She picked me because she knew I would always tell the truth. I said, "I was sleeping in the rocking chair, Danny was in your bed asleep, and Latrice was still awake. Danny left a lit candle by your bed and Latrice got in your bed and she burned a spot on her head." She looked at me and Danny and told Latrice to come to her. When she finished Latrice was walking around with her hair sticking up all over her head.

I was surprised that she didn't beat us. I couldn't believe it! I wanted to do a few flips! Danny wasn't talking to me that night she was angry. She kept saying that "I'm always trying to get her in trouble."

She said, "Next time when you finna get a whopping I'ma make sho I don't help you."

I guess she was referring to the beatings that I ran from and hid underneath the bed and she would sneak and feed me.

After Mother would get tired of chasing me, I would hide underneath the bed until the next morning. I remember one time I hid under the bed for almost two days and my sisters would sneak me food and feed me under the bed. It was cold and uncomfortable. I was hungry and anxious. I remember one day we got to go outside and we talked to Mrs. Gloria next door. She was an older woman and she gave me money every time I helped her with something. I'd spend hours at her house helping her out or eating, all of her baked goods.

One day she noticed we were in the house alone, she came over and fed us leftovers through the bars on the door. She always looked out for us. After about a year we moved into the house that my aunt once lived in next door.

Sometimes you have to knock down the brick wall just to get to the next phase, keep going! It's just a temporary condition that will prepare and mold you for greatness.

I'M ONLY HERE FOR THIRTY DAYS

Chapter 8

My Aunt Naple moved out of her property and my mom decided to move into the property she moved out of for more space. Mother had met this guy named Jodie. He was short with a light complexion. He had blue eyes and was a slick talker. I didn't like him because he always got into fights with my mother. I wished my dad was there to protect her. My dad would always just pop in and out, it was always good to see him. Every time Jodie came to the house, he would behave erratically, and it almost always turned into a fight between the two of them.

One day, Jodie came into the house, he was being loud and he was drunk. My sisters and I were in the backroom playing, we heard a loud uproar coming from the basement. I could hear my mother screaming repeatedly "Stop Jodie! Stop!" With every hit and pop that landed on the floor, I could hear her shouting; Danny wouldn't let us go down the stairs, I was so afraid, I felt like this was the worst fight of them all because I couldn't see it.

I could hear glass being broken and the table being knocked over, then I heard Jodie storm up the stairs, and my mother followed him. They continued yelling and shouting at each other but this time mother had a stick in her hand, and they were circling the table. I peeked from the corner in the hallway. Mother was about to pound him with her stick, she had blood on her shirt, her hair was all over her head, and scratches were on her neck. My mother always fought back when it came to Jodie, I knew that the blood on her shirt wasn't hers.

The next thing we heard was someone banging at the door, it was my Aunt Naple with a rifle. I felt a sense of relief and that I could come from hiding. She barged in and yelled "get out or I'm gone launch a bullet in yo ass," he ran out the door past my aunt with no problems. I didn't see him for a while. However, my mother was pregnant a month later with my little brother Lil Jodie.

There were nights, I would see my mother sitting at the kitchen table, gathered with her friends, her belly would be hanging out as she chopped and lined up cocaine and sniffed it. She and her friends would play cards all night, with mirror plates, taping and sniffing cocaine. I felt so bad for my unborn sibling because one night they overdid it and my mother went into premature labor. He didn't come right home after he was born, however, I kept asking my grandma why. She just kept saying that he was sick. Later, after overhearing a conversation my grandma had with her sister, I knew that my baby brother was born too early and that he was addicted to cocaine. My grandma went on to say that for him to be released he would have to come live with her. At eight years old it wasn't hard for me to gather that my mother's behavior and actions weren't good. I knew from the example of my stepmother Caroline that things should be completely different. I felt safe there and I got to see the other side of life, even if it was just for a little while. I felt wretched and so confused, I wanted my brother to come home with us, but I also wondered why grandma would take him and not us too.

If you don't love and respect yourself then you can't expect others to.

Chapter 9

After my brother was born, my mother's old boyfriend Carl, started coming back around. Carl yelled at my mother like he was a pimp. He was short, stocky build, and a drug addict. He always had a Colt 45 beer in his hand. When he came around he routinely argued with my mother. The arguments lasted all night; he would beat her up so badly that she would have to go to the emergency room. Afterward, she would be bedridden for days and sometimes even weeks, suffering from black eyes and broken arms. Every time they would fight Danny would always make us go into the back room.

One night, while we were asleep, mom was in our room searching for a few dollars that I had gotten from her company. I was awakened by the bright light that filled the room. I was half asleep when she sat on the edge of the full-size bed, gently enough not to disturb my sisters, she asked me where I hid my money. I could tell that she was worried or nervous about something, by the urgency in her voice. I always hid my money close to me, because I knew it would be safe and I would always know where it was. I reached under my pillow and gave her the balled-up few dollars. She said, "thank you, baby, I'm gone pay you back I promise." Then cut the light off and exited the room.

As I drifted back to sleep, I heard someone banging at the door. Then I heard a shallow but aggressive voice shout my mother's name repeatedly before she made it to the door. When she opened the door, I started to drift back off to sleep. By the sound of the voice, I knew it was Carl and he was talking loud to my mother, I could tell he had been drinking by the slurring of his words and the foul language he was using. My mother kept saying, "Carl can you please stop yelling my kids are asleep." I could hear him calling her names and becoming aggressive by the screeching sounds across the hardwood floor in the living area.

The sound of his heavy feet screeching across the floor and the force of my mother being shoved suddenly got closer. My sisters awakened and then I heard the bathroom door shut. We jumped out of bed and stood in the doorway of our bedroom. We heard him screaming in a panic at her and then moments later all I could hear was him smacking and punching her, repeatedly. I could hear the sound from him pounding her, I heard her screaming "Stop Carl! Please!" I felt so helpless because I knew I couldn't defeat him. All we could do was yell, "Stop it!"

I kept thinking to myself, what can we do? I couldn't help but feel that something was not okay, but I didn't know how to deal with it or how to make it better for her. I felt like I wanted to go in that bathroom that night and kill him myself, but Danny wouldn't let me. She grabbed me and put her hand over my mouth and desperately whispered, "shhhh." I stood in the doorway yelling, "Please stop hitting my mommy." At that point, I was fed up and I didn't care what happened to me all I knew was that we couldn't just stand there. All three of us started to cry and shouted "stop hurting my mommy" he opened the door to the bathroom and stood there in the doorway staring at us for a few seconds and then he walked out of the house. I was terrified, my heart was racing and pounding rapidly. We ran into the bathroom where my mother was leaning over the bathtub, blood was flowing out of her nose, she was crying uncontrollably and it was blood all over the bathroom floor. She told us to go to bed and get out of the bathroom. Danny and I gave her hugs and held her for as long as she would allow. I could care less if she beat me for trying to hug her that night. Mother shut us out of the bathroom and stayed in the bathroom for a while.

I grew terrified of Carl, but I still wanted to attack him when I saw him; he intimidated me because of how he beat my mother in front of us. I never said much but I was always thinking and every time I saw him after that I wanted to catch him sleeping. Carl moved in for a while and things got worse the beatings became more frequent and the police would be there more often. We dealt with fear inside our house and while having to put on a different face at school. We got to spend the weekends with our father and that was the best part of our week.

Get out before it's too late. You don't have to accept someone else's unruly behavior.

I'M ONLY HERE FOR THIRTY DAYS

Chapter 10

When we'd go to Caroline's house it was a different ball game. She'd let me be myself; which was "Miss Colorful Suzzy" referred to by, "Granny," she said that everywhere I went I had a big oversize granny purse with many colors and prints. However, when it was time to go somewhere, Caroline made sure I looked presentable. Caroline wanted the best for us, she wanted to help as much as she could. Caroline talked to my mother about us coming to live with them long-term, and my mother agreed. We lived with my dad and Caroline full-time. It felt so good living with her, we had everything we could need or ever want. Caroline always advocated for us whenever she felt that something wasn't right. She was there for us when we needed her the most.

One time, I had holes in my all-white "tennis shoes" everyone at school called my shoes "White girls." Every time I walked I would have to focus on not falling on my face because of the holes at the bottom of my shoes.

I could hear Caroline yelling at my father about "how he better get to the store and get both of my sisters and myself some new tennis shoes." I was outside playing in the mud with my little nephew when he stormed outside and said, "let's go, Tonya!" When my dad spoke loudly, I knew he was serious. He said, "It's no time for questions and just does as he said." He wore his black suede hat with the red feather on the side and listened to Al Green music as we headed to the store. It was a hot day, we had the windows rolled down, and my dad was sweating as usual. We drove to Payless Shoe Store, he got each of us two pairs of new shoes. He drove us back to the house and we ran inside to show Caroline our new "tennis shoes" as my dad drove away.

After a while, the house became crowded with my dad's side of the family. Caroline's family was from Nashville and she allowed my Aunt Clarisse and her children to occupy the 3rd floor. Danny and I shared a room with my oldest sister Salena and my stepsister and her son slept in the basement. My Aunt Clarisse moved out and my oldest brother moved his girlfriend in with their new baby on the third floor. Our house was full and we loved each other.

My dad began to stay out late more often. The arguments became more frequent with him and Caroline. I could tell that something was going on between them. I noticed her crying openly. She had the biggest heart, and I couldn't understand why anyone would make her upset. It saddened me. Caroline seemed frustrated and tired with the relationship she had with my dad.

One night, I came downstairs to get a drink of water and I heard laughing and doors opening downstairs in the basement. I peeked over the stairs to see what was going on and it was my dad coming through the door with friends. It was obvious they had been out drinking. He was loud and cursing. He was with a mysterious woman and his best friend Clive, I assumed he had just gotten off from work. He would sometimes stay out after work and have a beer or listen to music. After I heard the noise, I went back to bed. I loved to wait up for him when he got off from work, just to talk. He was a storyteller and I could tell he enjoyed talking to me, even if he was tired.

The next morning, I was awakened by the sun's glare and Danny's foot placed on my rib. I heard someone throwing what sounded like glass and yelling. I laid in bed and wondered what the argument was about? When I opened the door to see what was going on, I saw my dad leaving the house in a rage. When I saw him walk down the stairs, I felt like something serious had happened. I felt like it was the end of the good life for us if things didn't work out between my dad and Caroline. I wondered if he would come back later, but all I could see was Caroline packing his belongings and putting them at the door while cursing and crying.

I wondered if the argument was from the fun, he had the night before with his friends. Several weeks went by and my dad had not returned to the house but our family was still there. They had officially broken up. The house started to become too much for Caroline to keep up. We had no one to keep the yard cut, fix things, and keep everyone in order. It wasn't long before we were back at our grandmother's house and to wherever our mother stayed. The summer was ending and school would be starting soon.

I'M ONLY HERE FOR THIRTY DAYS

Chapter 11

Before Caroline sold the house, we went to visit her, and my dad picked us up for a few days. My nephew and I were sitting outside making mud pies. My dad drove up in a Burgundy 1999 Pontiac with a black drop-top. Sitting in the passenger seat was a familiar woman, she was light-complexioned, at least "5.8," all I could see was the back of her head. She had black and gold-streaked finger waves. She appeared to be well established by her demeanor. I figured it was his new girlfriend and that it was her car. I knew I had seen her before; she was the mysterious woman that came into the house with my dad and Clive at Caroline's house.

We met him at the car and then she got out of the car. She introduced herself and opened the back door for us to get in. Danny and I both had an awkward look of shock on our faces. She said, "Hi girls my name is Rosetta."

We entered the car and they told us we were going out to eat. During the ride to the restaurant, Rosetta asked us about school and what kinds of things we liked to do. It turned out to be a get-to-know-you session.

She seemed like a cool person but my sister wasn't open to her. I couldn't figure out why every time I answered Rosetta's questions Danny would sigh and swing her elbow into my arm. Danny remained quiet and to herself. I could tell she didn't want anything to do with Rosetta. Later, Danny told me that she felt like Rosetta messed up the relationship with our dad and Caroline. I was skeptical and confused, I didn't care too much if she was nice. However, I couldn't help but see how pretty and well-dressed Rosetta was. After our first meeting we hung out with her and my dad often, so we got to know each other a lot better.

Rosetta's house was nice, she lived in the Berkeley area of Saint Louis at the time. It was a white three-bedroom home that sat at the end of the block. Everything inside the house was very tidy and she kept everything in a specific order and manner. When we visited, she expected us to do the same. After a while, Danny hated it, because she didn't think it was fair for us to have to clean her house when we came over.

During our earlier visits, Rosetta and my dad spent a lot of time with us. Rosetta would always buy us nice clothes, especially for the holidays. During our first Easter together, Rosetta bought me a white fluffy gown with beads and ruffles. I had matching socks, and my hair was in Shirley Temple curls. I loved my dress, I felt like a princess. When

I reached the inside of the church, people were staring at me and laughing when I walked by. As service went on, people continued to laugh and point. I wondered what they saw, but I held on to the thought that I felt pretty before I entered the church.

What you put out is what you will receive in return.

Chapter 12

Moving from my aunt's property on Thrush Avenue caused my mother to move around a few times that year. It was the year 1995 I was 9 years old. Mother met a guy she had been hanging out with name Sean. He was short and had a coffee complexion with big shiny eyes. One of his legs was shorter than the other causing him to walk with a noticeable limp. He wasn't very talkative and seemed strange. But he had a nice appearance. Unlike the other men from mother's past, Sean worked full-time, had his place, and wasn't physically abusive. He was more established compared to the others. If he was a drug addict I couldn't tell.

We lived with him in his small apartment with my two sisters and myself. My little brother Jodie was adopted by my grandmother therefore, I didn't see him as often as my sisters.

Living with Sean was peaceful and more structured. We could watch cable television, eat well, and play. We could do what we wanted and be comfortable doing it. We received less severe beatings. My mother appeared to be healthier than ever. I never saw her doing drugs in front of us while we lived with Sean. She made sure we got to school daily, and that we had food on the table. We weren't hungry anymore. While we lived there things were peaceful. The lifestyle for us was complete and stable. We had a male figure in the house that took care of all of us.

My sisters and I slept on the couch and the floor, it was a plain one-bedroom apartment. The apartment was neat and very tidy. There was a place for everything. The apartment had one couch, a coffee table, a small recliner, and a television in the living room area. In the bedroom, there was a full-size bed, a dresser, lamp, and Chester drawer. The kitchen was small. It had a small table with two chairs. I remember the apartment being dry, warm, and cozy. Most nights, I could smell the aroma from my mother's soul food cooking in the kitchen. She had the luxury of cooking every night because Sean always made sure there was food for us. Sean went out for work every day in his blue 1989 Chevy pickup truck; my mother would see him off to work most mornings.

However, there were nights when my mother would be up arguing with Sean, they would always be arguing about mother not spending enough time at home. This would make her end up leaving sometimes for days. I always figured those nights were her party drug nights. At this point in my life, I knew that my mother did drugs and I understood what that meant. I paid close attention to the effects of her drug use and her mental illnesses. Sometimes her eyes would be dilated, she would be walking in circles picking up things that only appeared in her mind and she would be slurring her words. I knew that she was sick. I loved my mother regardless and I knew that when she came off the effects of drugs, she would be okay.

Sean rarely went out and I never saw him do drugs or drink excessively. He was really upset with my mother because she stayed out all the time. Most nights he would watch TV and talk on the phone while my sisters and I played games with each other around the house. Sometimes we spent more time with Sean than mother because she would be gone. He never engaged or interacted with us too much when my mom was around. He loved to tickle my baby sister Latrice and me. I was nine and Latrice was six. He would have us running back and forth pouncing on him as he sat on the couch before dinner.

We are defined by our actions, not by our appearance. what you appear to be is not who you are.

Chapter 13

One summer evening, after the fourth of July, it was almost dark and mother had been out for a few days. Danny was spending the night with our cousins. My baby sister and I were left at the apartment with Sean. I was outside playing in the complex and my sister was asleep. I got tired and I decided to go inside and watch TV. Sean was sitting on the couch watching TV in the living room. I came in and I asked him what he was watching and flopped down onto the couch. I glimpsed at the TV and he hesitated to tell me what he was watching but I could see that it was porn. I got up and went to the restroom, after leaving the restroom I went to the bedroom and laid on the bed with my baby sister. That was the first time I had ever seen porn or even took a glimpse at it. As I laid on the bed, I kept thinking to myself why is he watching that? It made me uncomfortable.

I laid on the bed for a little while then I heard him yell, "Tonya you can come in here and lay down and watch TV." I said, "No that's okay I will just lay in here." "I'm okay." He said, "Girl come in here and let her sleep." I got up, pulled the door closed so my sister wouldn't wake and took my shoes off, and laid down on the couch. He had just paused the porn then as I laid down, he changed the TV to the news. I laid down on the couch but I didn't stretch out because he was sitting at the end of the couch. I was wearing a pink and purple one-piece short suit. He tickled my feet; I didn't think much of it at the time, I was used to it so I laughed and giggled and kicked like my life depended on it. Then he rubbed his hands up my legs. At that point I felt guarded and weird, so I froze. I looked at him confused with fear like what are you doing. I couldn't believe that he was touching me in that manner. I kept asking myself is this okay or is it wrong? I had never been touched that way before, I became numb and frozen my stomach kept turning over; my heart started to pound, and I started to panic so I sat up.

He said, "Tonya it's okay, I know you're scared I'm not going to hurt you, I and your mother do this all the time girl sit down, this is how girls become women."

I sat back down on the couch, "Lay down!" He said.

I began to shake and all I could think was what is he going to do to me?

He said, "I'm going to be gentle; don't you want to feel good like your mother?"

I said, "No! I don't want to do this!"

He pulled me down by my feet closer to him and forced his way on top of me. He kept saying "I'm going to make you feel like a woman" repeatedly.

My body instantly went into shut down and I became stiff and powerless. He kissed my body starting at the neck. The instant his lips touched my neck I could feel in my stomach that this wasn't okay. I was overwhelmed by emotions and thoughts. My palms were sweaty and then I tried to push him off me.

I couldn't breathe!

He held my arms and breathed heavily.

"What is wrong with you? I'm not going to hurt you." He took my short suit off.

I screamed and yelled as loud as I could. "STOP! NO! NO!" Over and over again.

He hurried to put his hand over my mouth. "Be quiet before you wake your sister!" He grew angry and tired of me fighting screaming. That's when he put his arm over my chest and smacked me and said, "Shut up and relax your legs!" "It's not going to hurt you're going to become a woman you're going to feel good!"

I grew tired and effortless as he pressed his body weight on top of me to hold me down as he pulled my suit down, I cried hysterically. He unzipped his pants, I reached for the phone on the table and he snatched the phone and hit me on my knuckles with it and told me that was the last time!

He said, "Who you think you're going to call?" "If you even think about telling someone I will kill you!" "No one is going to believe you so stop it!" He continued with taking his underwear down as he forced my legs to open wider, he started rubbing his penis up against my vagina. Then he pinned his arms across my arms and chest, all I could hear was him moaning saying relax don't cry just relax as he slowly worked his way into my vagina. My legs were trembling, and my vagina felt like it had been stuck with pins and needles repeatedly and I could feel it stretching. The antagonizing pain I felt after he forced his way into my vagina words can't explain; then he rose a little only to release what was left of cum onto my lower abdomen. He got off of me as his sweat dripped down my body.

I felt weak. My chest felt restless and overworked, I felt violated, hurt, disgusted, dirty, sweaty, and ashamed. I curled up on the couch as tears rolled down my face. I watched as he got up, wiped himself off with a rag, ran bathwater, and laid clothes out on the bed for me. He came over to me and he said, "I am sorry that I hurt you, you are a woman now." He said, "Now you know you can't tell anyone about this" Then he showed me his gun case to remind me that if I told he would have to use it.

I sat there in fear with snot rolling down my lips and sweating because of the fear in my heart. My world had just been turned around and I didn't know what else to do. I didn't want to lose my life so I had to do as he said at least until I could tell someone that I knew would help me. Sean said "Tonya do you understand me?" I shook my head quickly, up and down, yes. After that he made me get into the bathtub with warm water.

My vagina burned on contact and I could barely sit or walk. I sat there in the tub crying hysterically. I felt so dirty and powerless. No one was there to protect me and frankly, no one could help me. Inside I blamed myself for not staying outside. Why did this happen to me? After my bath, I put on my nightclothes and Sean made dinner. I refused to eat anything. After dinner he cleaned the kitchen and went to bed and my baby sister was awake watching TV on the floor.

Instead of eating or anything I made a pallet in the corner of the living room and laid down on the floor. I didn't sleep that night all I could think about was what had happened to me. I laid down in fear that he was going to keep doing this to me. The thought of his scent and sweat made me ball up and cry all night. I knew that I had to get away.

Despite what negative feelings have come about, learn to love yourself anyway, nothing justifies rape. Some of the most successful people have been dragged through the mud face down but have succeeded way beyond their measure.

I'M ONLY HERE FOR THIRTY DAYS

Chapter 14

Over the next few days, Sean wouldn't go to work and he wouldn't leave me alone with anyone. Sean was responsible for getting us to school and making sure we ate when my mom was absent. My mom would call us to check on us but I couldn't talk to her, I had to pretend as if everything was okay because he would be right there. I had to go everywhere he went, and each time he would remind me of the gun and what he promised to do with it if I told.

One evening my mom was home and the three of us went to the Thrift Store to do some shopping. Sean was in a great mood he let the three of us buy clothes and toys. As we walked around the store, I kept thinking to myself that this was another thing that he was using to keep me quiet, buying me toys and clothes with the hopes of me keeping quiet. As if the threat of a gun being pointed at me wasn't enough.

In the store, he kept following me as I picked out my toy, he kept staring at me with his big dark-colored eyes and I could tell that he didn't want me to have a conversation with my mom by cutting me off. After we paid for our things, we went out to eat at my favorite place which was a restaurant called Ryan's. Sean knew that food would always make me happy. No matter how many plates of food, clothes, or toys I managed to get that night every time I saw Sean my heart would race, and any hint of happiness I felt would leave.

I didn't know how much longer I could hold it in. I was angry and I couldn't understand why my mother couldn't see or feel the hurt I was experiencing. How could I tell her? I knew that someone had to know what happened. I just had to wait for the right time, person, and place. I didn't know who I could trust or who would even believe me.

My mother continued to be gone for days and when she was home, she slept all day and stayed out all night. There wasn't a time to tell her or even hint to her what had taken place without getting hurt by Sean. I would beg her and my sister Danny not to leave with the look of fear on my face. I kept thinking to myself if they leave me alone with him again, I am going to be bait. I kept wondering if I told Mother would she believe me or what would she even say or do? I thought to myself, is this truly how girls become women? Is this a part of the process of transition to a woman? I was confused.

I knew I had to tell someone, but I didn't know how to come out and say what happened and how it would affect things. I wasn't 100% sure if I would make sense to anyone else.

*****

My dad seemed to be in such a great mood and happy to see us. As we entered the house, we unloaded our clothes. I remember feeling relieved as I laid in bed.

Dare to speak, your voice is what holds the key.

TONYA WILSON

Chapter 15

It was the first time Danny and I had gotten away and could talk privately. When we left it felt like a breath of fresh air and I could finally breathe again. My sister and I were up talking all night at my dad's house. We were just having girl talk it was just after midnight. My older sister was into boys at this time and she was sharing stories with me. I felt the need to share with her but the only thing I had to share was what Sean had done. It was all I could think about anyway.

I said, "You can't tell anyone." Repeatedly then she said, "Okay." the next thing I knew I said, "Sean did something to me."

"What Tonya?"

I said, "He put his thing in me"

She jumped up and said, "He did what? Tonya, do you know that's rape?" "Sean raped you!" She started yelling out of anger and she started crying, she said, "We have to tell Tonya!"

I said, "NO!" He will try and kill me if I tell anyone, this is why I didn't want to tell anyone!" Jumping up out of bed in frustration waving her hands she said, "Tonya it's wrong and he isn't going to do anything to you." "Tonya, we have to tell daddy, he will go to jail don't worry about what he said, he is going to do to you." She got out of bed and said, "I am going to go tell daddy."

I said, "they are asleep can't we wait until morning."

She said, "no we have to tell them now."

I started to get sweaty and nervous. I was afraid of what my dad would say and do.

She went and knocked on their bedroom door and woke them up. She said, "Tonya got something to tell you."

Our father came out of the bedroom and said, "what is it, Tonya?"

I was nervous as tears rolled down my face I mumbled, "Sean raped me."

I heard how crazy my father could get, but I had never seen him get that angry before. My dad said, "What girl speak up!"

My sister said, "Sean raped her she just told me about it!"

My dad became so angry he started to pace back and forth through the hall. Shouting, "Motherfucker!" repeatedly. Rosetta came into the room and sat next to me. She put her arm around me and said, "What happened, Tonya, did he do that to you?"

I said, "Yes and she told me it was going to be okay." She said,

"I am so sorry that you had to go through that."

Rosetta explained to me why it was wrong and what happened. I had no clue what rape or sex was at that time. I knew adults kissed, hugged, and got naked to show love but I didn't know what intercourse was until that night. Rosetta said, "Do your momma know? Was she there?" I said, "Naw she wasn't there and she doesn't know." "I was afraid to tell her because he said he would kill me if I told." "He is going to come after me."

Rosetta said, "well you don't have to worry about him trying to hurt you anymore I will make sure he goes to jail for a long time."

My dad made me call my mother and tell her. Although he had already talked with her in the other room, I had to face my fear and tell her what happened. On the phone, my mother seemed very calm but sad and disappointed. She asked me what he did and she asked me if I was sure. She kept saying, "I'm sorry and I love you okay." After I told my mother, Rosetta told us to lay down and try to get some sleep, she was going to the other room to talk with my father. Danny and I laid in bed bundled up together. Danny kept repeating in a soft whispering manner, "Why didn't you tell me, Tonya?" I shrugged my shoulders saying "I couldn't."

There is greatness in the power of strength.

TONYA WILSON

Chapter 16

It was a chilly morning about 6 am. Although we had only laid down for no more than 3 hours I couldn't sleep. I swung my feet around to the side of the bed, got up, and opened the door to use the bathroom. I could hear a lot of walking and I could smell the aroma of coffee. I walked out the door and the house was swarming with police and detectives.

Rosetta said, "Good morning, how did you sleep? Are you hungry?"

I said, "Can I have one of those donuts?"

She said, "Sure, when you get finished come in the living

room and sit on the couch this nice man is going to speak with you." She gestured over to the detective standing in the hall speaking with my dad.

I went on and prepared myself, I felt very nervous. I wasn't sure what was going to happen to the dynamic of my family. As I got dressed, Danny had awakened from all of the commotions, she heard me coming in, and out of the room. She said, "What's going on?"

I said, "There are a lot of detectives here and they're searching through our overnight bags." We had been up all morning and part of the night talking with the detectives.

By lunch, things had calmed down and then the phone calls started rolling in, family members, and friends of the family were calling to gather information. We were immediately taken away from our mother and placed with my dad. The detective said, "You don't have to worry about going back there, you girls are going to stay here with your dad for a while." My sister and I looked at each other nervously. I was worried that we wouldn't see my mother anymore. I kept thinking to myself what have I done.

I looked at the detective, I said, "Is my mom in trouble? Why can't I see her?"

He said, "Well, you see we have to talk to your mom about what happened and we just want to make sure that you're safe."

Shortly after being placed with my dad, he told me that Latrice was taken away also and moved in with my grandmother who had already taken in my baby brother Jodie from birth. I realized that we would be staying with my dad for a while.

The investigation was still underway. Rosetta told me that Sean had been arrested. She said, "You have to be examined by a doctor, this will help put Sean in jail." I was terrified I had never had a vaginal exam before, Rosetta and my sister kept trying to explain the process.

On the way to the doctor's office, I was shaking. Although the process had been explained I was still nervous. We arrived at the doctor's office and of course, It was a male doctor that was going to do the exam, I was instantly frightened and panicky. The room was white, there was a large exam table, two large monitors that were connected to the wall. Rosetta held my hand and helped me prepare for the exam, she told me that I was going to be okay. Rosetta was right by my side during the exam and throughout the process. The monitors showed the inside of the vagina and the doctor pulled samples for the detectives on the case and explained what they were looking for.

After the exam was complete, a court hearing was scheduled and that was all I could think about. I was nervous and I kept asking the GAL (Guardian ad Litem) which is an appointed lawyer that advocates for the minor's "best interest," I kept thinking, was he going to be in the courtroom when I had to tell what happened. The thought of this made my palms wet and my heart race. They kept telling me no, just a few people but I didn't believe them.

Living with my dad and Rosetta was a lot different compared to living with mom. Sometimes it seemed like a dream come true to be living with my dad but on the inside, there were some deep-rooted issues. Everyone was dealing with what happened and being overwhelmed by the sudden uproot. We were living in the city of Saint Louis. Their new house was a big spacious family flat-styled home. It was a full house with Rosetta's three older children including Danny and me. My stepsister Aasha had just had a baby girl, she was like a big sister to both of us. We talked but we didn't have much in common because she was a lot older than I was.

The house was always clean, organized, and just spotless. Rosetta was particular about the way she wanted things done around the house and made sure that we were fully aware of that. During our stay, because it was a vulnerable time Rosetta made sure that we were taken care of and that we had everything that we needed. Rosetta was very fun and outgoing. She made sure we went out often rather it was to the zoo or the parades during the summer. She took us under her wings everything she knew she taught it to us.

Living with Rosetta was a very difficult transition after being taken away from our mother. Everyone had to get to know each other abruptly and this took a toll on the new family dynamic.

With the new move adjustment and everything else going on, I couldn't focus at school or anything. For a while after the exam, I was in pain and it burned when I went to use the restroom, Rosetta called the doctor and he recommended that I take baths with ivory soap. For a while, I felt like the pain and the nightmare were never going to go away. I was hurt that I couldn't see mother for a while. So many times, I thought to myself this is all because I told. I wondered did I cause this all to happen?

My thoughts continued for as long as I could remember. I was worried that Sean would find me and follow through and use his gun on me. After he's sentenced will he get out and come find me to hurt me? Is mother upset with me? Because I told what happened and that caused the police to get involved and us to be taken away from her.

Chapter 17

Several weeks later, the trial day finally came. The silence and the nervousness took over my body and my mind I wondered what kind of questions they were going to ask me. I was nervous about having to walk into that courtroom and testify. My thoughts raced daily. I didn't feel as if I could tell them what happened to me. I was afraid to ever tell anything again. I was more comfortable with my inner thoughts. I was afraid that if I spoke something bad it would happen again. My inner thoughts were safe and it was all the control that I needed. I thought no one could punish me for speaking because I didn't have to. I kept wondering if I was brave enough to go through it. I knew he would go to jail and I would be safe. The car ride over to the Courthouse was long, we were all quiet, and no music was playing. We made it to the Courthouse, the building was massive, we had to go through metal detectors to get inside. We walked in and went up to the courtroom and then we just plopped down on the bench outside the courtroom. I glanced down at the new outfit Rosetta had bought me, just for court, it made me feel a little better about myself. It was a cute little blue jean and black dress with floral sewing, and I had on my first pair of black flats with two matching black bows. There weren't very many people in the hallways, besides lawyers passing through. The longer we sat there, I wondered, even though they made it clear that Sean wouldn't be in the courtroom when I testify, I felt like it was some sort of trick and that he would be somewhere nearby. I didn't trust any of them.

Meanwhile, my dad was pacing the halls, he was furious, his legs were shaking and his eyes were bloodshot. When he wasn't pacing, he was sitting and shaking his legs nervously. He appeared more upset and anxious than I did. My dad didn't say much to me, but he wore his feelings on his face that day. However, the two things he did say were that he loved me and assured me that I was going to be okay. Rosetta was sitting right next to me wiping the sweat off my father's face and rubbing his legs while holding my hand. As I waited patiently for the advocate to come and get us, I kept looking down at my feet as they swung back and forth as if I was on a swing at the park.

I asked to go to the bathroom, of course, one more reminder of what happened to me. I had to pee, and it burned. Dealing with the sensation of the burning and looking myself in the mirror

I said, "this is your fault." "You should have never told!" Then I calmed myself down and said, "it's not your fault that he did this to you, and he will pay just like sister said!" "You can so do this!" "Just tell them what happened and you will be okay!" "That's it!"

I went back into the waiting area and sat on the bench; part one of the trial was finished and then it was my turn. The lawyer came to the area where we were sitting and told me that they were ready for me. I got up and my dad kissed me on my forehead and then I went in. When I took the first step into the courtroom, I became intimidated by all the faces in the room. There had to be at least fifteen people sitting around the courtroom. Two people were asking me questions about the rape. My words stumbled at first when I had to swear in. As I thought back to that day, it became easier for me to explain what happened. The fact that he was arrested and he couldn't hurt me became my motivation to pull through the trial. It was difficult at times because the prosecuting attorney asked me repetitive questions and wanted me to go into detail on something I was ashamed to say in front of adults. The attorney asked me to tell her what happened and to walk her through what took place.

"Take your time," she said.

The lawyer asked me to explain what I was wearing, who was in the home at the time, their names, and their relationship. Most of the detailed questions were about the actual rape. I made it through the questions, but it was exceedingly difficult. Before I knew it they had no further questions and it was over. I walked out of the courtroom and my arms were sweating, I could see the sweat spots under my armpits. I was relieved that it was finally over.

TONYA WILSON

Chapter 18

After the trial, living with my dad started to change drastically. The bills became tight with Aasha moving back in. Rosetta and my dad got a small two-bedroom apartment in Ventura Village in North County. On the day that we moved everyone was in a horrible mood. Rosetta was busy getting everything organized and ready to go to the new apartment. My stepbrother and stepsister Aasha and Kwan lived there also. The apartment became overcrowded. After we moved in things became hostile between Rosetta, Danny, and me. Rosetta became frustrated with us and trying to keep the apartment clean and organized. My dad worked all day and Rosetta wasn't working and she would be with us most of the time. It was a tradition for us to sit and watch Showtime at the Apollo every weekend. Some nights, I would wait up for my dad to get home from work. I enjoyed talking to my father and he certainly loved to talk. We shared a love for sports.

When he would be at work, he would always call home to get the score.

"How many points does #24 have?" He'd ask.

I grew to love sports especially basketball. I learned about the players, the skills and techniques they use. Rosetta made sure we went to school faithfully every day and that we had the essentials we needed on a day-to-day basis.

During this time, we didn't see our mother often after the trial. While my dad was at work, I tried to stay outside in the apartment complex playing with my friends after school. When I did go inside, I knew I needed to stay out of the way and not get in trouble. On the weekends, I loved when my dad was home because he would cook for us, especially grand breakfast. We grew increasingly tired of Ramen Noodles, Polish, Pork N Beans, and Hot Dogs. I think as adults it's easier to feed children the same things because they complain or don't eat. When dad was home, we would get to eat ice cream, cookies, and anything else we wanted.

*****

It was a warm day outside and I went to take a walk. When I returned I heard Rosetta's voice from outside the apartment talking on the phone. I slid in the door and reminded myself that I am not allowed to have shoes on or sit on the couches in the living room area. I took off my tennis shoes. Rosetta loved to talk on the phone to her family about us during the hours my dad was at work. I remember eavesdropping and I heard her say.

"These little nasty bitches got to go back over there with

they crack-headed ass momma!" "Don't want to wash they ass, and then I tell the big black one to do something and shiid she looks at me like I'm stupid." "I can't stand these little bitches!"

To hear her speak this way about us to others broke my heart each time. I had hope that she didn't mean it. I wondered if my dad agreed with her feelings about us living with them. I knew it wasn't a possibility to go back to my mom, therefore, every time she would yell at us about something I'd try to correct the behavior she disliked. At the time, I felt like we had already moved around too much, and I didn't want to do anything that would jeopardize us not having a place to stay. I loved my dad and I wanted to be with him.

At school, however, I started to take my anger out by getting into fights. I wasn't doing my work, the kids were picking on me because of my clothes, shoes, and because I was sometimes quiet. One day, some girls that had been constantly bothering me followed me home and they were pushing me and I didn't want to fight. But this one girl kept messing with me, she called me dirty, and ugly repeatedly. I turned around, stopped, and rushed the girl. I grabbed the girl by her hair and book bag, and I began dragging and punching her around. The other kids were standing around instigating the fight. After that day I had enough and there was no turning back. I thought I could fight everyone. That girl never bothered me again and she was the "laughing stock" around the school.

After that, I became a bully. I felt defeated in every aspect of my life. So, I figured if I fought everyone and showed them how big and bad I was, nobody would mess with me. I didn't have new clothes or shoes like the other kids, but I became popular because I was known for fighting. I must have had at least seven fights, most of which I started. I was angry at the world; I kept my mouth shut at home and opened it wide at school. I was no longer going to be called a punk or the dirty girl.

While I was terrorizing the schoolyard, things had gotten out of hand at home. My dad and Rosetta were arguing more often, and Danny had grown boy crazy. She was no longer trusted in the house by herself. We had been keeping in contact with our big sister Salena regularly. Salena is our father's oldest daughter from his first marriage. We hadn't seen her much because of our age difference and because she lived with her mother. She was always around to comfort us when needed. When Rosetta left the house, she would clean and vacuum everything; polish every piece of furniture so she could tell where we walked and touched while she was away. She even put the phone cord up so we couldn't make any calls. One day Danny wanted to talk on the phone so she walked across Rosetta's vacuumed carpet and found the cord and made her calls. She put it back before Rosetta got home. When Rosetta got home, she immediately knew she had used the phone because of the footprints on the carpet and she beat us both with a cord that night.

Chapter 19

One night when Rosetta wanted to go play bingo, she couldn't find her bingo dabbers. She assumed that my father had thrown them in the trash, Rosetta searched around for the dabbers.

"Tonya and get in the trash and see if you see my dabbers." "Your dad threw them away so you have to go get them." She yelled.

Overwhelmed with frustration I headed out the front door and marched around to the dumpster with tears running down my face. It was dark outside and the only light that was on was from the bedroom. I could hear Rosetta coming out the main door.

I jumped over into the dumpster. It felt as if rats and other creatures were crawling around and up my legs. I kicked the dumpster and yelled out of fear that I had been bitten.

"You better stop kicking that dumpster before I whoop your ass," Rosetta yelled as she approached the dumpster.

"Girl quit all that damn crying, they ain't gone do nothing to you!" Look for it, it's in a white bag!" Rosetta coached. Standing in the middle of the dumpster, I saw a wooden stick, reached down and grabbed it, and used it to search for the bag with the dabbers in it! I got out of the dumpster and went back inside the house.

"Now I'm about to whoop your ass for kicking that dumpster and yelling."

Get out those clothes and bend them over! She yelled.

I stumbled in fear but moved very quickly to bend over the bed. She whooped me with her favorite weapon, the brown extension cord. I was screaming for my life praying for it to end! Finally, after it ended, she hurried me to get in the bath she had drawn.

Things continued to get hard with us living in the small apartment. We moved back and forth between my father and my aunt Clarissa's house. My aunt Clarissa would let us live with her during the times we couldn't stay with my dad.

One evening we had been living with Rosetta and my dad was at work.

Rosetta came home and swore that my sister had some boys in the house.

"You had that little boy in here, didn't you?" "I know you lying, cause I saw you!" "I'm gone whoop your ass." Danny replied as tears rolled down her face, "You not gone beat me, I'm going to my aunty house." Danny ran to the door. Rosetta became furious as she gathered our belongings and lined them up at the door.

"Well go!" "I don't give a fuck."

Danny grabbed my hand.

"Come on Tonya!" She shouted.

Danny and I left out the door with our bags and began to walk over to my aunt Clarissa's house. She lived on Imperial St. in North St. Louis.

It was late and freezing that night.

Danny and I had finally made it over to Aunt Clarissa's house. Filled with so much relief to have finally made it.

Danny knocked on the door and ranged the doorbell. Aunt Clarissa's boyfriend answered the door and cracked it enough just to show his face and he said, that we couldn't come in because my dad told Aunt Clarissa that she was in his business too much. Feeling lost and confused we walked to a pay phone at the gas station nearby and called

Salena. Danny explained to Salena what happened and she sent her husband Lamar to pick us up. We waited at the Phillip 66 on Chambers Rd and then Lamar pulled up in his Silver 1986 Cutlass Supreme blasting his music as usual. I hopped right in. Lamar cleared his throat and turned down the radio,

"Hey."

"What happened, what yawl doing out here?"

"Nothing." Danny replied as she hopped in the front.

I was excited to go over to Salena's house and to be off the streets. It felt like she was always saving us.

We headed over to my sister's house for the night. Little did I know that we would end up living with her more long-term.

I'M ONLY HERE FOR THIRTY DAYS

Chapter 20

Living with Salena for the rest of the year was extremely exciting for me. She spent a lot of time with me. I enjoyed going skating, making homemade scary movies, and throwing parties. Salena's house was like the equivalent of a frat house. Salena was the coolest sister ever. She was smart, sophisticated, energetic, and just a fun person to be around. Danny and I had so much fun living with her. Living with Salena was relaxing and comfortable. She made sure we got to school every day, that we ate, and that we were clothed. She loved us unconditionally and became accustomed to playing the role of a mother and a big sister. We had everything we needed and more.

Salena was married and worked full time at the hospital. There were times I went to work with her on the weekends overnight. She was my role model. Her house was huge; she had a full-finished basement, and a large backyard.

We had house parties and would go in the neighborhood and invite random people to the party. One time, we had a big party and we had people in line outside the house to get in. Lamar had turned the basement into a club. He had big speakers and DJ equipment. We charged people to get in. I was 11 years old, so the only thing I could do was dance. Salena taught me different dances. Salena had dance competitions in the basement all the time I would always win the dance competitions.

If we weren't having a party, we were going skating, to the movies, or downtown just to get out of the house. There was never a weekend that we just sat in the house. It was a great escape. At this point we didn't want to go back to my dad's and my sister didn't want us to either. However, my dad had threatened to call the police because we had technically run away. I could tell that his relationship with Rosetta was particularly important to him. We didn't want to sabotage my dad's relationship. Many nights when I lived with Salena, I would get to spend the night at my stepsister Connie's house. Her son Liam was around the same age as me and we played well together. I went over to her house to play with Liam all the time.

She used to style my hair all the time. One night she styled my hair for school the next day. Each night I stayed there I wrote little notes on a piece of paper about my day and placed them inside a black toolbox before I went to bed. I didn't have my notebook with me from my dad's house. I was always writing; it was a way for me to express myself.

Chapter 21

One night I was so tired I wrote a small note and fell asleep. That night was warm and cozy so I didn't sleep with the blanket on me all the way. I was on a pallet on the floor in my nephew's bedroom. I remember being asleep, it must've been late because it was very dark and quiet. I felt what felt like, big hands rubbing up against my legs slowly. Felt like something crawling. I thought, maybe I'm dreaming or that something was on me so I just move over a little. I fell back to sleep, then it started again, but this time rubbing my chest and my vagina at the same time then I jumped up with my eyes half-open and swatting. I looked around the room it was pitch-black but I could see this shadow kneeling over me, instantly felt hands covering my mouth, and before I could say anything they cleared their throat and whisper,

Shush! Lie down and go back to bed.

Suddenly I realized that it was Lamar. I couldn't figure out why he was in our room or why he was touching me. My mind started racing, flashbacks of what happened to me in the past caused me to panic. I was laying there wondering if I was just dreaming. "It's not real," I said to myself repeatedly. I rocked myself back to sleep and tucked the cover around my legs.

Then, I was awakened again, by rubbing up against my legs, I screamed "STOP! Now!"

He put his hands over my mouth.

"Shhh I'm not going to do anything to you!" He whispers. Then he leaned on me sideways, pulled up my nightgown, put his hand into my panties, and forced his finger into my vagina. Tears rolled down my face as I laid there thinking why is this happening to me again. Then my nephew woke up. Lamar immediately stopped touching me.

He said, "See I didn't do anything to you now go back to sleep." Then he went into the bathroom.

I cried the entire night I kept saying to myself it's something wrong with me. Why does this keep happening to me? I kept thinking was this wrong because it wasn't like the last time, he didn't put his "thing" in me. Should I tell anyone, is there anything to tell? I laid there confused and unsure of what just happened to me. My mind continued to race with all kinds of thoughts until I cried myself to exhaustion and fell back to sleep.

TONYA WILSON

Chapter 22

I got up for school the next morning and got dressed. Lamar kept playing around as usual with me and my sisters but I wasn't too excited. I looked at him in a whole different way. I couldn't figure out why he would do what he did to me the night before. I didn't want to be alone with him and I didn't want him near me. He went on like nothing ever happened. Even though I was so angry, I didn't want anything to mess things up with living with my sister. I figured if I keep my distance and make sure that I am never alone with him I would be okay. Nights when my sister would be gone, I would make plans to go visit Connie. I didn't want to go through the aftermath of telling and then we a placed with someone else. I just wrote about it.

That night after school I wrote a note about my day and I included what happened to me but I didn't go into details on the note I put in my note box.

As time went by, I was so happy and he never tried to mess with me again. A few weeks later, I went to visit my stepsister Connie to play with my nephew. My sisters called on the phone and said, "Tonya, we read your notes in your black box."

I asked her, "why she read my stuff? I told her that "it was personal." She said, "you wrote a note in there saying" "my sister's husband raped me." I told her that I didn't want to talk about it. She said well all we need to know is if it is true or not. I told her that I didn't want to talk about it, it's my business! Then my oldest sister got on the phone and asked me, "if it's true?" She said that I must tell her now. I said, "yes."

Then she told me to give my stepsister the phone back, they talked a while and then my stepsister tried to get more information out of me. I just didn't want to talk about it. I ended up staying with Connie for a while, Salena said I couldn't come back until she got it figured out.

I went back to Salena's house after spending some time at Connie's house. She took us to school the next morning as usual. I noticed Salena was becoming quieter and more reserved than usual. She didn't say much on the way to school.

At the end of the day, right before school let out, my dad showed up and checked me out of school early.

"Hey baby, what's going on?" I ran and hugged him.

I was happy to see him, but he wasn't so happy to see me. He was very upset as we stepped out of the school building.

We got into the car.

He said, why did you two run away, yall are coming back with me and Rosetta. I don't want to hear anything!"

When I saw him, I just put my head down because I knew I wasn't going to see my sister for a while. He was taking Danny and me back to his house.

Later on, I found out that my sister left her husband, and was going out of town for a while. I was devastated because I felt like it was my fault.

I'M ONLY HERE FOR THIRTY DAYS

Chapter 23

We lived with my dad and Rosetta briefly but after so many fights we went to stay with my Aunty Clarissa temporarily until it ended up being more long-term. I was entering middle school when we lived with my Aunt Clarissa. There was no more shuffling back and forth because Rosetta no longer wanted us back over to her house to live. Father would come over to my Aunt Clarissa's house when he and Rosetta weren't seeing eye to eye.

Living with my Aunty Clarissa was probably the most life-changing aspect of my entire being. It was a cool time in my life. My Aunt had a 3-bedroom home with a full basement and backyard. My Aunt was very loving and caring; she was a sweet woman. Her health wasn't the best at this time, she had a home nurse, and she needed a lot of help. She would do anything for anyone if she could. She allowed us to move in with her and her children. At the time she had her daughter and her son living with her. They each had a bedroom, my sister and I stayed in the back den. Danny was the type to hang out; she ventured off into new things away from me. She and my cousin Qualita were hanging out with their basketball coach a whole lot. Qualita always talked to me and kept me singing. My cousin Qualita was so talented she could rap and sing. She was always writing songs that kept my mind off other things. I walked to school every day. I'd come straight home after school and either go ride my bike or play out in the garage with the basketball. Meanwhile, my sister was being picked up after school by my cousin Qualita's basketball coach so I started asking questions and he agreed to let me join the team. I was so excited I loved basketball more than my sister and I could play a whole lot better than she could. He started taking me to games and practices. His name was Coach Willard he was someone that I looked up to, he was successful, smart, really nice, and he cared about us all. He did a lot for my sister and me. He turned me into a beast on the court and showed me how to play the game. I did what I needed to do at home and school just so that I could play basketball; everything I did was for basketball. I lived, eat, and breathed basketball.

What I loved was on Saturday mornings my Aunt would get up and make homemade biscuits for breakfast. She had special syrup that she used for the biscuits; everyone in the family enjoyed her biscuits.

It wasn't long before we moved to the city. We moved into a family flat it had two-floor levels. We had three bedrooms upstairs, one bedroom downstairs, a kitchen, and a living space. It was a spacious home, we enjoyed living there. Shortly after we moved in a family next door moved in, we enrolled into the school around the corner. I was still playing basketball and I played basketball with every boy on our block every day. I was occupied with basketball and school. When the school year started I met a lot of friends and I started playing basketball for the school. There were a few girls that I thought would be good on my other basketball team called the Lady Bulls with Coach Willard. I brought them along to join our team. That basketball team meant the world to me and everyone on it did as well.

We grew to be great friends and we hung out all the time and we had great chemistry on the court. That same chemistry won our games. Coach Willard was involved in every aspect of our team. He taught us how to raise money for our team uniforms. He always made sure we ate after our games and that we had plenty to drink during our games. He was there for everything we needed. He even got involved in our personal lives individually and did what he could to help out. He kept us off the street, we didn't have too much free time because he kept us productive. We joined the African American Role-Model Program. It was a group of "black Muslims," we would meet often for events. We would go to six flags, and they gave us lots of encouragement. We had movie nights and other outings. Through this program, it gave us hope and resources that the community could count on. It was a place where children like us could be occupied with something positive.

My sister had slowly drifted away from the team. I had become the captain of the team and I was the one whom everyone followed. I was goofy and always joking around with my teammates. There was another girl I met at school;

she was a girly girl her name was Lisa. She could sing, I hung out with her and we started singing together. Lisa and I participated in talent shows and at family reunions. We would sing everywhere. She brought out the shyness in me and I was singing a whole lot more. I started to believe in my voice and have more confidence. She was tall and I liked hanging out with her and her family. Her mother was always encouraging us. I enjoyed hanging out with her so much that I invited her to join our basketball team but she didn't play long.

She wasn't very coordinated and she had butterfingers. She was funny on the court but she was a beast on the microphone. When basketball season was over, I joined the step team at the recreational center. Ms. Catrina was good friends with Coach Willard and some of us joined her team. It was fun, we were in many competitions and talent shows.

I learned discipline from her she was a "Black Muslim" as well. She was very educated and strict. There were lots of things to do with our step team as well, we would have girl nights, sleep over's, skating parties, and movie nights. When I did have time at home, I just helped out around the house and took care of my Aunt.

I played ball outside in the front yard and jumped rope. It was the year 2000 and people were saying that the world was going to end. I was 13 years old. There were killings, break-ins around the neighborhood and people started to steal cars.

The neighborhood had gotten rough. My Aunt was tired of me and my sister living with her and she called my uncle's to help discipline us. My Aunt was already sick and she couldn't get stressed out and having us there was becoming too much for her to handle. I just tried to stay out of the way but that didn't last too long.

I'M ONLY HERE FOR THIRTY DAYS

Chapter 24

One day, as I walked home from school I saw everyone outside including my neighbors. My 14th birthday had just past so I was eating a cupcake from a friend at school. As I approached the house, I saw a white van that had Ashbury Children's Home on it. I went into the house and a woman named Andrea introduced herself to me. She told me to sit down and that she needed to talk to me but we had to wait until my sister came in. I said, "ok" and then my cousin said, "I just saw Danny get off the bus, she coming up the street now." She got up and I met her at the door

"Hi, I'm Andrea from Ashbury Children's Home. Nice to

meet you." She said.

Danny and I both looked at Aunt Clarissa in confusion. My Aunt said. "I can't do it any more girls; I need a break. I am tired so you girls are going to have to go with Ms. Andrea."

Danny asked, "to where?

"To Ashburn Children's Home," Andrea said and started explaining the group home program in detail. Danny started to cry and then the caseworker explained that it was only for 30 days. Danny got up and ran out the door full speed up the street. I ran after her yelling, "Danny." Repeatedly.

Ms. Andrea was right behind me.

Danny finally stopped after about 4 blocks, and she said, "No, I'm not going to no home. I'm not going! Tonya, don't you know what that means?" "We're going to a lockdown facility with others girls that don't have families. We won't be able to see our family or anything." She explained.

I said, "I know but it's only for 30 days, We can do this. This is just for Aunt Clarissa to get a break."

She agreed. We headed back towards the house and met Ms. Andrea as she was walking towards us. When we made it back inside the house, we packed a few things and loaded them into the van. It was so humiliating and embarrassing.

During the car ride over Ms.Andrea talked to us and she explained that she was going to be our caseworker with the Children's Division. She continued to explain to us how it worked and what the facility was like.

I was angry with my Aunt for the way she did us, but I was even more upset with my sister. I felt like we wouldn't be leaving if she hadn't been skipping school. Not being able to go home didn't bother me too much because I knew it would only be for 30 days.

I'M ONLY HERE FOR THIRTY DAYS

Chapter 25

For thirty days living at Ashbury went well. When we arrived at the unit, they went through our trash bags of belongings and confiscated all of the sharp and liquid items. The only thing we could carry into the rooms was clothes.

They split us up, my sister went on one side of the unit and I went on the other side. We got to make two phone calls a day, we had chores each day, and we had to ask to move throughout the unit. They explained the rules again and then they showed me my room, we all had roommates. My roommate was the boss hog of the unit. She was a force to be reckoned with but little did she know I was too. I kept my mouth shut because I didn't want anything to prevent me from going home when my thirty days were up. Every time someone asked me any questions I would always say "I'm only here for thirty days."

My sister and I were called the thirty-day chicks because that's all we knew. It was indeed something I felt ashamed of but I knew I had to focus on what I was going to do for me to get out of there. My sister stayed in her room most of the day and only came out to eat. I talked with my roommate and a few other girls, but I was a little cautious because those girls couldn't hold water.

They were also aggressive. There were at least ten fights in the unit during the thirty days we were there. There was only one girl that my sister and I bonded with and her name was DJ. She was short, dark-complexioned, loud, and bossy. She had a kind heart and she was there for us whenever we needed to talk. All three of us fell in love with a particular staff person named Ms. M. She did so much for us that showed us that she cared. She loved the girls in the unit but she was closer to the three of us, especially DJ. DJ had been there the longest and their bond was stronger.

Ms. M was the sweetest woman and she was very funny. She seemed to have it all and she was willing to share whatever she had with us. During this time, we were taken to school in the van with the company's name on it. Sometimes our caseworker would drive her car to take us to school. Some days when school was over, she would let us sit in her office with her when she was on campus. Ashbury looked like a campus with four different buildings inside. It had a big black gate around it. The campus was very dark, it didn't have many lights. They had a lock-down unit and an open unit for girls and boys, a cafeteria, and a behavior school. Most of the girls in the unit attended school on campus. Sometimes we would go there for recreation and if the weather was nice, we would go outside and play on the playground. That was a time when we could mingle with the boys. The girls in my unit were drawn to me because all the boys were cool with me. After all, I could play basketball and I would kick butt on the court. Instead of me going out with them, I hooked them up with the girls in the unit.

When it was time for us to leave, I packed my bags and got my personal belongings from the staff and I said my goodbyes. It was the day after my birthday. The girls in the unit were sad that I was leaving, but it was bittersweet for me. Andrea came and got us and we went to my Aunt's house.

We all sat down and my Aunt gave us both hugs. We talked about our progress and what we plan to do better with each other and at the end of the meeting my aunt said, "I can't do it any more girls."

I have to think about my health, you girls are just going to have to stay at Ashbury permanently. Danny and I looked at each other and we hugged and cried and screamed "why!"

We tried begging and pleading, but she kept shaking her head no. I remember getting into that van feeling betrayed, unwanted, and not loved. I felt alone and completely hurt. I was mad at the world. I will never forget my sister and I picked our heads up wiped our tears and we said, "it's just me and you, we all we got." That was our motto.

We walked back into Ashbury with our trash bags of the rest of our belongings. The girls were excited to see me but

I felt humiliated because for 30 days all I kept saying was I'm only here for 30 days.

From that day on Ashbury was my new home and family. I never looked at my family the same after that. I felt like they just sent us to the wolves and nobody ever cared. We stayed at Ashbury for the rest of the year.

Want to know what happens after the 30 days?

I'm Only Here for 30 Days

  Part 2

Coming Summer 2024

TONYA WILSON

ABOUT THE AUTHOR

Tonya C. Wilson is an Entrepreneur/Mentor/Advocate for all foster youth worldwide from Saint Louis, Mo. She grew up in a single-family home and experienced some life-changing events which lead to her and her siblings being split up throughout the foster care system. She not only grew up in the system but had the wonderful opportunity to work in the field as well. She is a strong advocate for all youth. Tonya has been working with at-risk youth for more than 15 years. She graduated from American Inter-Continental University with a degree in Business Administration/Marketing and is a career student. Tonya started writing at the age of 14. Her memoir "A Way Out" was Re-released in 2013 as "I'm Only Here for 30 Days" also in 2021. It is a testament to all youth facing challenging life experiences.

www.ingramcontent.com/pod-product-compliance
Lightning Source LLC
Chambersburg PA
CBHW070456100426
42743CB00010B/1637